MANAGEMENT FOR COMPETITIVENESS

Dr. Doris Martin

MARTIN MANAGEMENT BOOKS

ISBN 0-9615541-8-5

Library of Congress LC 91-090340

Martin Management Books, Box 119, RR #1,
            Wailuku, Hawaii 96793

TABLE OF CONTENTS

INTRODUCTION

The challenge of the century for corporations that are based in America, recognized equally by those based elsewhere in the world, is the challenge of competitiveness!

The consequences of the failure to compete successfully will have negative aspects of great magnitude, not only for individual firms, their shareholders, and personnel, but also for the economy of the nation in which their headquarters is based.

Competitiveness is THE issue for multinational firms...but also for firms that are primarily domestic, as foreign ownership, joint ventures, and investment from foreign sources escalates. The pace of change has quickened. Today's dynamic business environment shifts quickly and in often unexpected ways, while pressures from competitors are steady and unrelenting in most industries.

There is really nothing new in the foregoing statement. By now, competitiveness as THE major issue is well recognized by the CEO's and other leadership of most individual corporations. However, the question of HOW to effect such competitiveness is another matter.

To be successful against stiff competition, each corporate management must maximize its essential

aspects and develop its organization to peaks of
performance that are sustainable over time... It
thereby creating a new norm within the firm. It
is the responsibility of every executive and manager to develop his firm to this peak potential
performance, and to insure that maximum progress
is made along the way to that goal.

Every business has goals identified as key areas
of strategy which are critical to the survival of
that firm. Three of these are shared by all
businesses. They are the goal of profits, the
need for productivity, and the necessity for overall performance. All are essential for competitiveness. They are the central focus of this book.

Corporations are trying a variety of diverse
approaches to build their competitiveness. Slash
and burn internal restructuring has taken place
in many firms, involving also the revitalization
of processes, and the renewal of the corporate
culture, often utilizing technology as a major
support tool.

This effort to identify the most appropriate response for each firm is a critical one for those
managers seeking to revitalize their operations
internally in an ever shifting, aggressive, and
rough and tumble environment. However, most of
these efforts appear to be widely fragmented, in-
complete, and incorrectly focused.

This book attempts to bridge-the-gap between
much management, business, economic, and organizational theory and the practical management
settings in which they are utilized by major
corporations today.

It is also based on the direct management, administrative, and consulting experience of the author.
The aim of the book is to clarify certain management aspects essential to competitiveness, with
the expectation that it will be useful to managers
at various organizational levels who seek to maximize their corporate potential and attain and remain competitive.

Six philosophical values undergird the selection
of materials, systems, and suggested actions to
enhance competitiveness and maximize profits, productivity, and performance. They are:

First, that a corporation must be viewed and
operated as a unified and integrated whole, and
not as a collection of independent and unrelated parts.

Second, that ideally each manager and employee
of the organization contributes something different toward the total common effort, without
either gaps or duplication of effort.

Third, that results oriented techniques, methods
of control, and motivating and facilitating processes, must be applied to all parts of the
organization, both vertically and laterally,
not just in one area such as manufacturing.

Fourth, that continuing progress toward competitiveness goals will be sought primarily
through organizational modifications, with technology in a supporting role.

Fifth, that to maximize competitiveness, the
systems, techniques, and tools suggested should

be utilized simultaneously in a parallel
approach.

Sixth, that competitiveness efforts must be
an ongoing process which requires constant
monitoring for problems throughout the firm.

Raising the competitiveness level of the firm,
and bringing the profits, productivity, and performance levels nearer their optimum level in
the most effective and efficient ways, is the
problem the book addresses.

The organization of the book reflects it's major
emphases. First, the nature of competitiveness
is examined. Next, the various considerations
of profitability in competitiveness are explored.

The next three chapters concern themselves with
corporate organization, productivity, and total
performance.

Finally, a summary concludes the book, suggesting
guidelines for developing systems and actions
which will support corporate efforts for sustained maximum competitiveness.

CHAPTER I
COMPETITIVENESS

What is competitiveness? Competitiveness is a contest between rivals seeking to secure business or a portion of the market under pressure. Competition can be foreign or domestic. Is your corporation competitive? With whom do you compete in each key area?

Fear of shakeouts, decline, and bankruptcy are motivating corporate change in many cases, while goals of increased growth, profits, and market share spur others. Corporations say they want to:

.be an effective competitor in the U.S. and globally.

.improve profitability and achieve solid value for investors on a quarter to quarter basis

.be a world leader in their industry or products ...to be a product leader

.maximize assets

.improve productivity throughout company

.become results oriented

.achieve excellence and quality

Within the corporation profits and value creation
issues are combined with a recognition of the
need for support within the firm, leading in turn
to strategic planning for company growth and internal organizational development.

What do corporations themselves mean by competitiveness? To be competitive means different things
to different people. To some it is an action, to
some a result, to a few it is a process, and to
still others it is an attitude. CEO's among the
Fortune and Forbes listed firms have provided a
sample of meanings:

"Competitiveness is WINNING...It is holding your
own against the best in the industry globally.
It is sharing successfully in a broadened field.
It is not eliminating the competition entirely,
because only the consumer can do that.

It is to excel ...to pick the right markets.
It is to outrun, outshoot, and outmaneuver the
competition.
To get into fighting trim. To be a growth machine
both lean and flexible!

Competitiveness is having a CAN DO attitude. It
is pride in our country and in our products, with
no apology.

It is sometimes being energetic, impatient, de-
manding. It is facing reality squarely.

It implies a rate of return on capital and creating more value than another owner because of a
special expertise.

Competitiveness is managing the whole effectively

on an ongoing basis. Winning customers and markets
against the competition...going THEM one better.
Taking-back our market share if we have lost it.
Getting and staying competitive by increasing our
productivity at least 10% a year."

To attain greater competitiveness involves increasing profits and market share within an increasingly complex environment through a planned
visionary strategy of what CAN BE DONE based on
current forecasts of corporate internal and external conditions, the quality and expertise of
managers and workers, overall level of operating
efficiency and effectiveness, level of commercial-
ized innovation, speed, quality, and productive
efficiency of production processes, consumer –
sensitivity and sophistication of marketing, and
other factors. These factors, in turn, must be
supported with unified and integrated structures
and processes which have been fine-tuned within
a flexible and simple set of policies and procedures, geared to the dynamic fast pace required.

In framing a competitive strategy, corporations
have unique circumstances. Setting corporate
strategy is an individual matter. Perhaps one of
the most important considerations is what constitutes success in that industry at this time.
Another is, who is your best competition? This
information is vital and basic to any strategy.
Among the many types of information that might be
useful is competitor products, pricing, use of
technology, distribution channels, suppliers,
market trends, consumer projections and others.
Who is the world-class competitor who sets the
standard for others to outdo in your product
fields?

Beyond industry, competition characteristics, and

products, other factors which must be considered
are management and labor , cultural heritage,
growth patterns, organizational and structural
factors, market maturity, financial circumstances,
and many others.

Once a competitive strategy is set, the right priorities must be identified which build on basic
core business strengths, with results constantly
monitored and revised upward periodically toward
optimum performance.

It is essential in implementing the competitive
strategy that the atmosphere be dynamic, aggressive
fast, and optimistic. Fear of bankruptcy or take-
over can provide an initial motivator, but must
evolve into a positive approach for the long haul,
otherwise the perpetual gloom and anxiety will
defeat the competitiveness goals.

Beyond this level, there is an "X" factor in competitiveness! In such cases, competitiveness is
an extention of an emotional involvement which
lends the utmost enthusiasm, relentlessness, per-
sistance, and even ruthlessness to the attainment
of the goals set.

Some analysts credit Japan's aggressiveness to a
national economic goal which stems from their
humiliation in the last war...an economic goal
to which many of their business, government, and
political leaders are committed This type of "X"
factor nationalism is, of course, even more
threatening when it appears to be working to the
unfair disadvantage of other nations.

Thus, within industries and individual firms, the

use of emotion combined with aggression toward
any major competitor is being increasingly recognized as one way to provide a competitive
edge. Other ways are through visionary leadership within the firm and a commitment to corporate and American ideals.

Regardless of motivation, corporations must base
their strategies on the expectation of white-
knuckled competition in the years ahead, as investment, profitability, productivity, and geographic development expands throughout the world.

It is interesting that there is a common pattern
for most firms who first recognize the need to
become more competitive in a fluctuating economy.

First, firms retrench, consolidate, sell off
assets, realign structure, and slash personnel
in various restructuring moves to cut costs
and increase cash flow.

Second, the firm typically will deploy some remaining resources to try and stabilize the new
corporate structure, and remaining managers and
personnel.

Finally, attention is given to corporate competitiveness, productivity, profits, and performance , involving new and improved products,
new strategies, and new or retrained personnel.

In the search for competitiveness, most firms are
instituting multiple interrelated efforts at improvement, building stronger and more responsive
structures and processes which can internally
support expanded competitiveness activities and
result in a dynamic and integrated organization.

To determine exactly what changes to make, in -
ternal assessment and appraisal processes have
become increasingly important, often involving
the intense and highly critical scrutiny of units
and processes by executive committees. Businesses
that can be made profitable are fixed; others are
divested. Subsequently, strategies to obtain
corporate objectives are then devised.

When corporate competitiveness is the strategy,
internal and external problems which affect the
strategy must be identified and met head-on.

Externally, the problem of high competition and
market share, through which profits are attained,
may involve inadequate benchmarking of the competition, poor products, late timing to market,
or inadequate consumer and cultural assessment.

Internally, the inadequacy of the internal organization to support and augment market performance
must be recognized. Spotty efforts at corporate
improvement can backfire. Fragmented and uncoordinated or conflicting systems can defeat efficiency goals. Fear of change itself can defeat or
delay needed action until it is too late to gain
advantage. Low producing research and development
or misplaced research or production priorities
can mean poor products that are late to market.
Technology that is inadequate for managerial decisions or manufacturing purposes can defeat the
firm's bid to gain a competitive edge.

Although there are many different variations in
corporate cultures, structures, and organization
among the competitive and successful firms, there

is general agreement that competitive organizations have most or all of the following
characteristics:

Characteristics of the competitive firm:

- the corporation is profitable
  It has attained product cost leadership.

- it holds a significant market leadership position.

- it is productive, with effective and efficient processes in a lean structure.
  Attention is given to the "fit" between the
  strategy, organizational characteristics,
  market requirements, and other factors.

- all assets are prudently managed; costs are
  kept down.

- in the competitive corporation, the focus is
  is on RESULTS for the organization. Human resource considerations are secondary...but they
  are also considered most important. Accountability is managed and controlled. Results are
  the basis for evaluation of individual performance, and also for evaluation of units
  and groups. Performance expectations are set,
  goal directed behavior is encouraged, and
  management-by-objectives systems are used.
  Priorities are set in every area in confor -
  mance with the competitiveness strategy.

- competitive corporate strategies and planning
  focus on long-range optimization of performance
  with all that this entails in a particular

organization, internally and externally.The
company resources should be allocated to
maximize desired competitive results, and
controls set for goal attainment.

. in competitive corporations, direction is
given to change in cultural norms and values
from the top. Organizational competitiveness
values and strategies are expressed daily,
and are extensively utilized in manager training and committee sessions where they are woven
into daily operational guidance. The total
corporate culture reflects competitiveness
goals, priorities, and objectives.

. competitive corporations are responsive and
operate at an accelerated pace. They are flexible but have a definite structure and form,
and are stable.

. competitive corporate strategies and goals
have evolved in depth and sophistication. Many
procedures operate on multilevels within firms
to insure communication. Policies, systems,
structure and processes are integrated where
needed for better goal attainment. Knowledge
of change procedures which have proven workable are a part of corporate knowledge and
policy.

. managers and employees have positive can-do
and even gung-ho attitudes. They are also
shrewd and effective in what they do. They
have strong ego structures and can cope with
stress without resorting to self-destructive
or conflict behavior. They are committed to
organization results, to which they have also
contributed through planning and participation.

- competitive corporations have a sense of
  public responsibility on local, regional, and
  global levels.

- they have formed successful alliances or cooperative agreements with relevant outside
  institutions such as banks, industries, and
  governments, within legal limits.

Impressive as successful competitive corporations
are today, they will need all of their abilities
sharpened to retain their positions in the decades ahead. Indications are that competitiveness
struggles will hinge on some of these factors:

- at present there is a slow down of economic
  growth throughout the world. Therefore the
  anticipated level of sales is not expected
  to rise dramatically. Competition for existing sales will intensify, and internal
  efficiency will be come even more important
  in gaining profits and market share growth.

  American firms will need to look to exports
  for growth in many cases, due to economic
  instability at home in the domestic market.
  Some firms will gain a major share of profits in new oeverseas markets. But for both
  multinational firms and smaller firms, competition will intensify.

- capital will continue to be needed for investments and a variety of internal competitiveness needs, i.e. technology and research
  in high v alue added products. Global growth
  will depend on efficiency in maintaining it
  ...finding the best resources, establishing
  a market position when a real opportunity
  exists, and not appearing to be or be -

ing vulnerable to others. Firms with a
heavy debt load cannot be competitive.

.realistic and critical corporate self-evalua-
tion against the world's best in your industry
is essential. The focus should be on:What is
the competitor's source of advantage? Compete
on that source of advantage first. Is it price?
Product quality? Better product positioning in
world markets? Better customer responsiveness?

Internal factors, such as speedy product commercialization, the advantageous use of cutting
edge technology, new products, new markets,
the stability, reliability, and speed of
company systems so that strategy can be implemented effectively on local levels as
opportunities are identified, are all im -
portant.

.Sustained competitiveness and market share
are dependent also on a largely unrecognized
factor of the perception of the company by
those on the outside...customers, governments,
financial institutions and others. Not only
the corporate image, but the corporate reality
should reflect credibility and reliability
in both its products and its dealings.

. the shrewd gathering and fast use of information on market trends and opportunities helps.

. the quality and abilities of executives, managers and employees in competitiveness values
and their capacity for continued learning is
vital.

. Finally, companies who want to be competitive
will have that "X" factor that insures a strong
commitment and drive toward maximum effort.

CHAPTER II
MAXIMIZING PROFITS

Maximizing profits is the primary goal of management, and is what competitiveness is all about. Solid profits permit pursuit of corporate long-range goals, provides funds for investment, and dividends for stockholders. Profits means success for executives and managers. Profits means growth, and also the ability to maintain an advantage in the capital market against LBO's. Liquidity and financial slack, when needed, can make the critical difference between success and failure,

Businesses fail because management fails to insure adequate profit levels. In today's cut-throat economy, both foreign and domestic, maximizing profits is essential.

Profits are increasingly unstable. World economic conditions, plus trends toward shorter product cycles, shorter production runs, shorter time in market for new products, brought about by more sophisticated demands from consumers and short-term production advantages, result in this instability.

To achieve a financial competitive advantage, cost, revenues and all other relevant corporate factors

must be carefully managed at the same time. Many
corporations today have taken stringent measures
to insure their firm's profitability by radical
measures in the areas of cost control, products,
and customer responsiveness.

Let us review some essentials about profit before
proceeding further.

Profit is the difference between income and ex-
pense. No matter how high expenses are, there is
a profit if revenues are higher. Conversely, no
matter how high revenue is, expenses must be lower or there is no profit. Profit is closely tied in
with corporate growth, market share, and quality
products.

The corporate goal in the profit area is to exceed
your competitor's financial results.

In terms of competitiveness, the following con-
cepts should be understood:

. profitability is the central measure of performance in a business. A profit goal might
  be expressed as "increasing the return on
  capital investment by 10% after taxes within three years.

  Profitability is expressed as earnings per
  share, return on investment, profit to sales
  ratio or other.

. market share is usually identified as market
  standing, i.e. 51% of the market, or expressed
  as in unit volume, or as dollars.

. productivity is usually expressed as inputs
  to outputs ratios, i.e. 10 units per worker
  per 8 hour day.

- financial results are expressed as new issues
  of shares, cash flow, working capital, divi-
  dend payments, and capital structure.

- worker performance is often described in
  terms of data on absenteeism, turnover, and
  number of grievances filed.

- corporate public responsibility is measured
  by the amount and kind of financial donations
  per year, or the number of public activities
  to which time has been given.

- the amount of risk a company is willing to
  take at any time is diminishing due to the
  competitiveness factors and instability of
  markets. For example, diversifying into
  business activity which may be more profitable may be discouraged because of aver-
  sion to risk-taking. All factors must be
  weighted carefully and experienced judgement
  consulted.

<u>Boards of Directors</u> are, of course, primarily in-
terested in profits. However, these should be pursued in ways which do not weaken the firm and its
long range competitive position. Profits should
ideally be pursued through product innovation and
management of a growth policy founded an good
procedures, rather than in manipulation and acquisitions and mergers.

In this connection the major problem of excessive
debt must be mentioned. The company must resist
becoming heavily leveraged. Excessive debt is
dangerous to both the health of the company and
to the perception of its health in the eyes of
potential investors, banks, and competitors.

Traditional sources of business capital, banking
institutions, will insist on more secure loans,
although public stock offerings are still a
source of financing.

In order to keep that safety net needed against an
economic downturn, companies must not be heavily
in debt. Equity financing may offer possibilities
or a combination of debt and equity financing may
offer the most advantageous combination. Ratio of
debt to total capital should be well below 50%;
many firms have ratios of below 20%.

Under these circumstances the company will remain
attractive to new investors, will retain its
flexibility in dealing with rapidly shifting circumstances and markets and will appear strong.

If additional sources of financing are necessary
new sources should be investigated, such as the
vast pension funds available, selected foreign
financing, or arrangements with other companies.

Management gets profit in various ways, i.e.
through operating efficiencies shown in return on
equity, return on assets, net profit margins based
on operating factors, and on manager, marketing
and sales skill.

Profit growth also occurs through various contributing factors, such as the quality of the
corporate strategy and how well it is implemented.

Effective competitive strategy is based on corporate goals in relation to unique competitive
factors. This analysis, plus the way the company
works to develop ideas, manage crisis, solve
problems, identify and eliminate the many barriers,

delegate resources, and manage operations and
people, all indicates the level of competitiveness which should result in high morale as well
as increased market share.

Maximum effectiveness must be obtained in the
total business, with all efforts of the individual
units consistent with the goals and strategy of the
organization, The primary priority must be clear.
For many firms, it is profits. This goal must be
kept in mind in all policy and operating matters.
Even so, the company may find itself in a crisis
situation when profits are all important.

The Crisis Situation

When a company is in a crisis situation, profits
and cash flow are all important. In such situations CEO's will stress profits above all other
goals. They will:

- make changes only in areas that will have the
  greatest profit impact, i.e. slash and burn
  cost cutting, marketing, production, massive
  restructuring.

- make the organization highly results oriented,

- seek labor concessions, business selloffs,
  plant closings, inventory reductions and other
  actions.

- take personal control of corporate cash, and
  must approve all expenditures.

To get the business back on track, they will:

- invest in core businesses and those making
  profits, and divest others less efficient.

. make new acquisitions carefully.

. tighten corporate control of all internal factors,

. increase efficiency and consolidate resources,

. invest in marketing and advertising to create
a demand for products,

. strengthen production with changes in tech -
nology.

. hire a few excellent managers with turn-about
capability who can identify problem areas.

The combined immediate effect of improvements in
efficiency, divestment of unprofitable business
units, slashes in numbers of managers and employees, and other cost effective changes, plus added
marketing effort, should provide profits for the
short run.

Many companies have been faced, at some time, with
just such a crisis situation. One of the better
known of these is the Chrysler Corporation.

Chrysler Corporation was short of cash and on
the verge of bankruptcy in 1979 when Lee Iacocca
negotiated a loan from the U.S. Congress. This
firm held a third rank share in the domestic auto-
mobile market, and insignificant overseas sales,
and made errors in judgement as it tried to compete with General Motors. The following year, the
company made a profit which enabled it to pay
off the debt.

The survival strategy which worked for Chrysler

included:

- . work force cuts from 156,000 to 74,000.

- . gaining of United Auto Worker concessions
  which reduced wages to $1.5 bil, 28% less
  within three years.

- . sell-offs of businesses that Chrysler didn't
  need for core strength, including those under-
  performing overseas.

- . the number of company plants was cut from 52
  to 36, a 1/3 reduction.

- . money was saved by changes such as inventory
  reduction, transporatation , and a reduction
  and standardization of parts from 70,000 to
  40,000.

As a result of these and other measures, this
company has $900 mil in cash in January, 1983, up
$1 mil from 1981.

Subsequently the priorities of the firm were then
able to be changed to an emphasis on products
and markets, which will help determine the longer
range future of the firm.

Since this time Chrysler has again experienced
financial crisis. However, the example cited remains an excellent one of a turnabout that
worked.

Maximizing profits is essential to any business.
Since the price of the products is mostly de-
termined by the marketplace...the competitors
and customers, management must make a difference in

profits determination through control of costs,
efficiency, and effectiveness of operations in
various relevant areas which will have profitable results. Among examples of the latter
are :
     unique products.
     repeat sales , building loyalty to a product
          or brand name.
     unique positioning of products in high ex -
          posure areas, domestically or overseas.

     high volume sales on low margin products.

     cost effective product design.

     effective and efficient manufacturing pro-
          duction or unique high quality products.

     speedy and effective race to market with new
          product.

In analyzing how to become more profitable, it is
essential for every firm to identify exactly how
it now makes its money. Then, what does it do
with the money it makes? Does it invest in plant
or research and development? Pay dividends and
give salary adjustments?

How effectively does the company use its resources
to make additional profit? How much interest is
paid? How much return on each investment? How much
debt service must be paid each month?

To make a company more profitable, finances must
be managed carefully and shrewedly. Financial information must be timely and effectively used by
the financial staff and managers , where applicable.

Although more profits can usually be obtained by

investment in the marketing area in sales force
or advertising, such expenditures may also wipe-
out any profits made. Caution is therefore needed in this area as a profits technique.

Many techniques to increase profits are available
to business however, and are used in a fragmented
way...some by one business and some by another.
Those listed below are worthy of serious con -
sideration by companies wanting to maximize profits
and most can be used simultaneously.

Techniques to Improve Profits

Improving corporate profits depends on reducing
costs, increasing efficiency and effectiveness,
and creating a company which can compete successfully in it's marketplace in growth, profit, and
sales.

Even firms with a strong growth goal must balance
this emphasis against the costs of such growth.
Often the internal costs of coordinating, integrating, and supporting growth efforts on local,
national, and world levels can be extensive and
expensive. Growth strategies, as well as other
strategies, must be carefully assessed against
anticipated profit, and also against the demands
of that growth on the internal structure.

Integration and some centralization of functions
can be cost effective, efficient, and productive.
The avoidance of duplication is essential. However this value also must be balanced against
the need for local responsiveness and the role
it plays in the profit picture.

Corporations go overseas primarily to get around
high tariffs which lessen profits on exports.
Combined with the economic downturn in the U.S.
market, new sales and profits are welcome. The
anticipated financial investment in overseas
plant and facilities can be much less costly and
less risky when joint ventures and partnerships
are entered into and are successful.

Within the corporation, one of the most essential
requirements is a financial staff that is
fully qualified. Various specialists will be expected to create ways to make more money legi-
timately, as well as the more commonly accepted
techniques of cost accounting, budgeting, fore-
casting, break even analysis, volume data, product
and pricing. Financial aspects of administrative
policies and procedures fall within their re-
sponisbility, as does also the improvement of data
for the management information system, upon which
decisions are made. Data must be timely and centralized.

The financial staff has the reponsibility of
tightening, focusing, and controlling the system
as may be necessary. A continuous program of internal audits can be used for monitoring of results and to identify problem areas. Responsibility
for each aspect of the financial program must be
fixed.

Profit oriented firms always have a tight program
of cost reduction or cost containment, together
with efficiency programs, which will produce savings. Savings will be balanced against growth
goals and other high priority items . One financial goal is to bring the cost of products into
competition with foreign products.

Some efficiency actions commonly practiced by
corporations include:

. lower debt service which eats profits monthly.
  Keep corporate debt low.

. reduce management levels in the organization.

. close non-productive businesses, plants, and
  divisions.

. reduce headquarters administrative support
  staff.

. eliminate unprofitable product groups.

. purchase materials and resources at the least
  cost for desired quality. Scan sources
  around the world for value.

. consolidate functions where workable.

. conserve energy.

. scan transportation and distribution areas
  for savings.

. utilize economies of scale in manufacturing.

. standardize product design, lower number of
  parts, but keep it flexible.

. purchase substitute materials that are of
  comparable quality for existing products.

. shorten production cycles, get products to
  market faster.

- shift emphasis from inspection and repair of
  error to prevention of error.

- review physical layouts and logistics for
  efficiency and needed integration.

- update production equipment, office equipment,
  and communications equipment for advantage
  in cutting edge technology.

- review all work. Do only the most necessary
  work in the most efficient ways.

- use resources and capacity fully.

- keep inventories down. Consider just-in-time.

- train managers in cost cutting and other
  areas as may be necessary for their effective
  functioning in financial areas.

- invest funds only in ways that will bring in
  a profit, i.e. support the most profitable
  units in the company with the resources they
  need. Invest overseas for additional sales, if
  more savings can be realized in tax breaks,
  lower labor costs, and economies of scale.

- when potentially profitable investment opportunities are found, optimize investment.

- give a faster response to market conditions
  and shifts.

- update product design to reflect consumer
  ideas.

- increase demand for your products by:

lowering prices.
narrow product line.
increase distribution outlets,
segment consumers and tailor products more
    precisely'
motivate salesmen to sell harder.
invest in more advertising or in more sales-
    men if justified by potential profits.

. get competitive information on segmented
  markets. Compare your product value and
  cost with that of the competition. If indicated, improve your product and sell it for
  less on the basis of benchmarking .

. listen to customer complaints and suggestions.

. get manager and employee suggestions on all
  aspects of potential improved efficiency and
  profits.

. innovate for profit and savings, i.e. in the
  R & D race for new products to market,
  in risk sharing new pay-for-performance personnel incentives, and in legitimate money
  making areas.

. control budgets. An analysis can reveal problems involving personnel :

unwarrented overtime.
excessive absenteeisn, sick leave, health cost.
personnel shortages.
idle time, down time of managers or workers ,
excessive time spent in committees,
manager failure to follow financial procedures
    such as bid procedure, failure to take
    warrented discounts and many others.

. problems of any kind usually mean lost time,
  delays, and therefore loss of profit. Identify
  and solve them quickly. Problems may be in
  production delays, late vendor-supplier delays,
  reject or rework rate, problems of shortages
  in products or raw materials, excessive conflict
  problems between units or individuals, integration problems vertically or laterally,
  problems in the information or data areas ,
  and large inventories which must then lead
  to price cuts to enhance sales with further
  profit loss.

Other suggestions to improve profits:

. make it a rule to get the lowest cost and
  highest quality in everything possible,
  from deciding where to manufacture a product to buying parts and components.

. analyze break even points and reduce them
  systematically, by more closely meeting
  market requirements, simplifying operations
  or consolidating them, reducing employee
  levels.

. develop effectiveness and efficiency in
  cross-functional and integrated management
  between R & D, manufacturing, and sales, and
  linking units with functions and systems.

. use corporate resources to the best advantage
  of the company, organization-wide. This in-
  cludes profit from any unit.

. make profits a cornerstone of strategy.

. make capital commitments in plant and equipment, obtaining the most competitive possible.

. make acquisitions of other businesses carefully. When made, integrate all aspects of the
  business fully and as quickly as possible to
  avoid costly delay.

. keep financial role of the company strong and
  control firmly.

. review executive pay scales and bring them
  into line with corporate and competitive
  scales, or justify carefully.

. review quality levels of products. How high
  a quality is appropriate for that product
  in that market,must be appropriate but at
  the same time not cost excessive.

.strive for the best corporate strategy at the
  least cost in all problem areas or conflicting
  value areas.

Devising a Profit Maximization Program

To devise a profit maximization program for an individual corporation, the following steps are
suggested:

. determine the present corporate position on
  profits. To do this, the financial staff
  should use internal audits, breakeven analysis,
  budget analysis, productivity analysis in each
  work unit (see productivity chapter), and an
  analysis of problems which have a financial
  impact. Although you may be making a good
  profit, the objective is to determine whether

you could be amking more if you were operating at optimal efficiency and effectiveness.

- it is important that each functional unit be
  analyzed for additional profit potential and
  also for profit leaks. When a suspected leak
  is found, identify the problem, the probable
  cause, and fix it. When the total organization has been tightened up and profit leaks
  fixed, profit will be nearer maximization.

- in addition, since managers know their own
  units or businesses best, ask them to identify warning indicators of future profit
  problems...such as slow moving products,
  budget overruns, production delays, customer
  complaints, or any others. Get manager suggestions to improve procedures. The idea is to
  prevent profit deterioration before it gets
  serious.

- make profit performance a cornerstone in the
  corporate strategy. Preferred practices to
  maximize profits must be practiced throughout the organization.

- focus on the best ways to increase profits:

  - decrease costs through efficiency and
    cost reduction, especially in manufac-
    turing, marketing, and personnel areas.

  - locate unprofitable areas and make them
    profitable or divest them.

  - manage financial resources of cash, in-
    vestments and costs, as well as debt,
    in the most advantageous manner.

. control financial, budget, and cost areas
  and manage them shrewdly.

. invest more in marketing and motivate harder
  selling.

. detect profit erosion in internal corporate
  processes, the way the company does things
  which inevitably causes work to be redone or
  redesigned. In considering any process,
  start with the END RESULT you wish to obtain
  and involve all those concerned in getting
  that result. When a cost of a product is
  the end result, compromises will need to be
  made by departments and suppliers until the
  cost is met. That cost must insure profitability of that product.

It should be noted however, that profitability
will not always be the deciding factor for individual products. In some cases, groups of product will be considered more important to market-
share than the profitability of any one item.

There are many reasons why profit is not closer
to being maximized in many firms. Much depends
on managers throughout the company on every level
in decentralized locations and how well they make
decisions with costs and efficiency in mind. The
overall strategy must be known and the efficiency
focus followed. Training is important here.

But for most firms, an analysis of the individual
corporate situation, reviewing operations in all
units to detect profit erosion, continuous
monitoring of operations, instituting programs of
financial control, fixing profit leaks, together

with some of the other techniques identified in
this book should move any company nearer
profit maximization.

Continuous attention to the tie-in of profit
with corporate strategies for competitiveness
is essential for success.

CHAPTER III
ORGANIZATION

Essential to making the corporation competitive
is to make the structure lean, efficient, and as
effective as possible. Attention to processes and
tools improvement cannot help an organization that
is ridgid, slow moving, cumbersome, and awkward in
decision-making. Immediate savings can be made
by structural efficiency moves, as well as the
facilitation of support for subsequent restructuring .

In considering the best structure for the more
competitive organization, there must be a "fit"
between strategy, goals, and the core capabilities
of the firm.

Some firms need responsiveness to the market.
These decentralize their structure. Others need
to stress efficiency and tend to exploit scale
economics. These centralize their operational controls. There are many organizational variations.

The most important factor is the need to get the
"fit", which is the best strategic requirement of
the industry and business, meeting the ability of
the firm to provide that requirement

All firms today need to consider efficiency,
effectiveness, market responsiveness, and ulti-

mately total performance.

Before considering structural variations, let us
review organizational fundamentals.

Organization Fundamentals

The structure of an organization is a formal and
informal network of authority and power relationships that are formed between individuals and
groups and their corporate roles. Managers and
executives hold line authority; staff is advisory
or coordinative in responsibility.

In considering the organization, think of it as
a total entity, a whole system, with various subsystems within the total, which has a climate or
culture of its own. This corporate personality is
viewed by external groups and is the image they
see.

Organizational structure is the concrete means by
which people are delegated responsibility and authority for decision-making, and are held accountable for results they attain or fail to attain.

Major functions which must be considered along with
structure are:

- administration, including planning, research,
  development, personnel, public relations etc.

- finance, including comptroller, treasurer, tax
  and audit functions.

- production, including manufacturing and engineering.

- marketing, including sales.

In redesigning the organization, many firms today have adopted the"contingency" approach which
combines the various elements in an organization
to provide that desired "fit" for corporate
goals at any one time. In this form, different
parts of the organization will have different
structures, with authority either closely or
loosely held,

The major criteria for selection of organizational
design is whether it is the best design for the
tasks to be accomplished and the goals to be reach-
ed at that time... In other words, does it work?
Does it make the firm more competitive? More profitable? What does it take to be competitive in
this environment and market, with our firm?

Both organization structures and processes must be
adequate to support corporate competitiveness
efforts, ranging from production and product redesign to process and systems creativity,to build
in organizational responsiveness and flexibility.

In seeking the right structure, the basic forms
that follow are usually considered.

- <u>the bureaucratic structure</u> is the simpliest
  form, usually developing from a simple pyramid
  with a chain-of-command and a ridgid structure
  in which policies,procedures, and form guide
  behavior. This structure is highly centralized
  and task oriented. Information is obtained
  vertically from chain-of-command, and laterally
  from committees, task forces, and liaison personnel. Highly detailed rules and ways of behavior predominate.Companies using this form
  usually have little market competition for
  its products.

. <u>the centralized functional structure</u> is somewhat more complex. In this form the organization is based on functions, i.e. finance,
marketing, personnel, production, research and
development, corporate relations, and others.
Authority is based on function, although there
is also a high degree of centralized decision-
making, leading to conflict between line and
staff authority and functional authority.

When an outside competitive threat is seen,
change tends to occur in the form of more
vertical information, further centralization of
authority, and the use of project teams and
committees. If functional authority no longer
seems adequate, change is most often made to
the divisionalized structure.

. <u>the divisionalized structure</u> is even more
closely related to corporate survival issues
in an environment perceived as competitive
and complex. The focus is clear, most fre-
quently by product. By creating divisions, size
is made more manageable. Each division can be
different from others. This form accomodates
the search for growth through diversification.

Problems with this structure stem from the
very independence of the divisions. Divisive-
ness and competition for internal resources
and political influence within the organization are fostered. Employees and managers will
often identify with the division and not with
the corporation as a whole, as much as in the
previously mentioned forms. When divisions
become too large due to diversification, there
is no longer a basis for this grouping and may
force a change to a product emphasis.

Separate divisions operate as cost or profit
centers, which leads to more reliable information flow and controls. A greater need
for integration and coordination is seen.
Typically, management-by-objectives programs
are used, as are task forces and training
programs. Information flow is vertical and
horizontal.

This form is widely used in American business.
It solves many problems, but creates its own
new ones.

.   <u>the conglomerate structure</u> is used by multinational organizations. Divisions operating
transnationally are called conglomerates. The
divisions have unrelated products. They may
be in a number of industry categories. The
corporation as a whole grows through mergers
and acquisitions. Sales of divisions in the
hundreds of millions is not uncommon.

Simple integrating devices are used. The head
office staff is small and highly professional.
The subsidiaries or units are independent.
There is a loss of benefit in economies of
scale and coordinated effort but gains in
smaller, competitive, and manageable units
themselves which are closer to the market
place. The basic unit is the profit center,
not the functional department. Therefore
there is less general coordination required.
The primary area of interdependence is between the product area divisions and the
corporate headquarters.

Because of the wide diversification of industries and products, much autonomy is permitted
in strategy and operations.

Corporate control is exercised through evaluation and finance and other economic aspects of unit plans, the allocation of funds,
budgets, requests for expansion aspects which
fall outside their unit, rather than in
direct participation in formulating the unit
or product marketing strategies.

All divisions have an acute need for reliable
data on which to base decisions.

. <u>the subsidiary company</u> is even more independent from the central office, with the exception
of financial reporting through a modified
management system.

Subsidiaries usually have multiple objectives.
Their markets are different from one another
and of differing complexity. Functions within subsidiaries are often duplicated without
concern for overall costs. They have different
kinds of people working for them, in conformance with their requirements.

Since the units are more autonomous, the need
for an integrative mechanism declines. There
may be less need for extensive information
flows , but the information they do need must
be current and reliable. Subsidiaries do their
own thing, relatively unrelated to others,
except for the balance sheet or when there
is a crisis which affects the entire firm.

In all cases, increasing marketing pressures are
forcing corporations to look at and try out alter-
native forms of structures which may be both par-
tial forms and temporary in nature. Three of these
are the project team, product management, and matrix.

- <u>project teams</u> consist of a group of assigned
  specialists, drawn from diverse disciplines
  within the total organization. They work under
  a manager selected to accomplish a specific
  objective. The primary purpose is to accomplish
  the goal or task, which goes across divisions
  or functional units. Team members are accountable to both their functional head and to a
  project manager. Both the manager and the team
  operate independently of the normal chain-
  of - command. Teams are used for a variety
  of specific purposes,and to tackle problems,
  especially if the time frame is limited.
  They can be most effective as a structural
  resource.

- <u>product management</u> occurs most often in organizations with centralized production,
  marketing, finance, and personnel functions,
  where a need exists to integrate product
  marketing vertically and laterally. The product manager is the integrator and can wield
  considerable power in the organization. This
  form is especially useful in food companies
  where brand names are prominent.

- <u>matrix organization</u> consists of a vertical
  hierarchy structure combined with a lateral
  structure to legitimize duel relationships
  and roles. It is established primarily to deal
  with complexities in the work environment,
  replacing informal horizontal coordination with
  formal structure. It is especially useful in
  a project approach. Pressures are high to
  accomplish task. Groups are expert and self-
  motivated. Multinational firms often use this
  modified form to coordinate production and
  geographic territories. Others have found it
  too complex for use.

Common Problems Related to Organization

Deciding what structure to utilize as a basis for corporate restructuring is a major task. Firms decide to seek solutions because they have problems with existing organization structure which is proving to be inadequate for the competitive thrust in the market place and the laboratory and factory today. There are no simple answers and no single key to the best competitive structure . Individual circumstances must be analyzed and problems identified,

Also, since we are dealing today with a constantly changing environment,solutions must be considered to be temporary and made to fit the combination of variables that management needs to deal with today.

Competitiveness relies on a good supporting system and organization, policies and procedures. If the effect of these organizational realities is negative or inadequate, the quest for corporate competitiveness is doomed to failure in the long haul. Does your total organization support the achievement of competitiveness goals or block them? Some of the more common organizational problems are given below.

- an organization with many levels, top heavy and costly central staff, and centralized decision making, will have greater costs in personnel and facilities, more distorted communication, and delays in decision-making, with a loss of competitive advantage. A flatter structure is better.

  However, centralization, with fewer levels is effective for tight control of resources, decisions, or policy.

. chain - of - command problems include reporting to more than one boss, such as in a matrix
  organization, which divides authority in decision making. Another is too great a span of
  control for one manager, common in lean firms
  today. The informal diffusion of authority
  which this creates can delay and distort
  decision making and encourage power grabs
  between units or businesses.

. authority, responsibility, and decision problems
  can occur with frequency between central headquarters and the decentralized unit, as each
  tries to carry out its responsibilities.
  Usually headquarters sets policy guidelines
  and the decentralized unit operates within
  them, and is monitored and evaluated on the
  results. Differences of opinion, caused by
  local market conditions and perceptions,
  occur. And, if profits are required to be
  shifted back to a central pool for the best
  use of the company as strategic resources,
  resentments will build.

. ridgid organization structures, the tendency
  to bureaucratize, is accompanied by slow decision making, excessive detailed rules and
  procedures. Usually there is too much written
  communication required, and almost no lateral
  communication.

  a related problem lies with the management
  information system (MIS) . Due to the
  standardization of data forms, information
  that does not fit is deleted. Often it could
  be useful to management for competitive
  reasons. Other routes should be found. Cut
  backs on computer printouts is appropriate.

- exploding corporate growth often adds pro -
  blems in the proliferation of projects and
  functional departments which are attached to
  an existing unit or division. Attention must
  be given to regrouping to the most logical
  location according to work flow patterns
  which will have the greatest advantage for
  both the work to be accomplished and personnel
  morale.

- excessive activity but no work results...work
  productivity performance below expectation...
  is a problem in corporations who have over
  reacted to human relations approaches by allowing excessive time to be spent in committees
  and other informal groupings, in informal in-
  teraction with those not directly involved in
  problems or work discussed, and in an excess
  of reports from subcommittee groups.

Touching base with others should not be an
unstructured activity. Remedy lies in firm
direct supervision, clarification of roles,
and results-oriented evaluation for both
managers and employees.

A related area is no work results due to an
excess of internal conflict between units or
individuals. The reasons and communication
channels must be examined and resolved.

- lack of sufficient lateral linking and cooperation across division or unit lines is a
  serious organizational problem for those with
  competitiveness goals.

The problem itself stems basically from over-

specialization in larger corporations in
which there is also some rigidity of structure. Any unit or profit center who is geo-
graphically isolated, can quickly lose the
big picture of the organizational compe -
titiveness goals and strategy. Polarization
of vested interests among units may develop,
with secrecy, hostility, and paraniod behavior. Isolation is reinforced by the use of
vertical chain-of-command without establishing a lateral structure of any kind.

Integrating procedures, work flow, and tasks
efficiently is a pressing issue in most firms.
Not everything needs to be integrated. In-
deed there is no corporation that is com-
pletely integrated, nor needs to be. However,
what does need to be linked or integrated,
usually needs it critically for the efficient
functioning of the firm.

Analysis of factors involved in whether or
not to integrate should include considera-
tion of the integration objectives, time
span covered, tasks involved with products,
skills, processes, customers, etc. Also the
people involved and their qualifications,
the pressures for integration themselves,
the technical or plant requirements, the
form that integration will take, and how it
will be managed and carried forward.

Vertical integration has gotten much more
attention from management than lateral linking. More attention needs to be paid to this
area to counteract fragmentation and ineffi-
ciency

Ideally, interdependent relationships will

need to be established among product, functional, and geographic management groups
for the best interests of the competitive
corporation in sharing resources, expertise,
information, and implementation cooperation
in specific geographic or other instances.

Integration may be needed at:
   .senior management levels to review whole
        company systems, problems, financial
        aspects, strategies and priorities.

   .product group level management to review
        geographic , technical, and marketing
        results, solve problems, and respond
        quickly to local level considerations.

   .specialist or technical level managers
        may meet to review problems and in-
        tegrate procedures.

Integration, both vertically and laterally,
cannot be over-stressed as a contributing
factor in successful support of competitiveness goals, allowing the efficient, fast, and
effective functioning of the firm, as it re-
solves production, work-flow marketing, and
people problems among diverse units.

. lack of an effective and efficient top level
   corporate planning system, which top management consideres a major tool, is also a
   major problem with strategic impact.

Once the organization mission has been set
and goals established, the most advantageous
plan will tie -in both department and indi-

vidual performance goals with results
evaluation, usually a modification of
the management-by-objectives design.

Lacks in the planning systems of most firms
center around the lack of planning procedures at different corporate levels, lack of
an information and data base for the analysis of alternatives in the planning process, and the lack of an adequately skilled
planning support staff.

.   redundancy, similar work being done by more
    than one department, is wasted effort,
    wasted time, and wasted resources. Unless
    there is a strategic reason for deliberate
    redundancy as is sometimes done for alter-
    native results in research or other area,
    redundancy increases costs dramatically.

.   inconsistent policies and practices is
    another common problem area. A formal or-
    ganization chart that has nothing to do
    with the reality of actual working rela-
    tionships, inequitable titles, assignments,
    and financial compensation for executives
    can destroy morale and authority.

    Restructuring and mergers, currently part
    of a massive shake-out, are now so fre-
    quent that the organization chart assumes
    even more importance, as an aid in locating
    where authority and responsibility lie
    for decisions.

.   policy-making apparatus and procedures
    which are poorly defined and unclear can
    cause confusion and delays.

This is especially true in roles and relationships between Boards of Directors and
top management. Lack of formal procedures
between CEO appointed Boards and their CEO
for evaluation of performance is common.
Staff assistance for the Board to support
work is usually inadequate.

At the present time, Boards are being held
increasingly responsible for the overall financial health of their organizations. Members
should be of high quality and thoroughly oriented to the company and current problems,
with responsibilities established.

- top management job responsibility must be
  clearly defined. In competitive corporations
  which stress the values of profits, productivity, and performance, top management
  must not only verbalize values...it must also
  act and implement these values.

- information and communication system design
  should be monitored to determine who should
  have access to what information, at what
  times. Much time and effort is wasted when
  managers are swamped with printouts and data
  which is not needed directly.

- accountability and evaluation of work results specifically directed toward the accom-
  plishment of competitive organization goals
  is largely missing. The use of results oriented evaluation systems, when combined with
  appropriate incentives, insure the desired
  high quality focused behaviors.

- failure to develop a widely known organiza-

tion articulation, voice, and image within the firm. This cultural climate and
communications problem is one of clarity and
emphasis...sometimes with only one key idea
repeated and reinforced.

. formal systems and procedures for reviewing,
  updating and replacing physical resources,
  lagging technology, methods, and processes
  will lead to competitiveness gains.

  Internal systems to monitor and evaluate organizational effectiveness are often inadequate for the needs of the firm. Systems
  should be established with clear goals and
  functions. Training may be needed for how best
  to use any system established in minimal time.
  Systems should be cost effective, fit the
  organization structure, and support the goals
  and values to be furthered.

. the continuing of all temporary teams, task
  forces, and committees should be provided for
  so the work accomplished has the proper follow-
  up, implementation, or dissemination.

. flexibility, the ability of the corporation
  to respond quickly to opportunities or to
  pressures in the marketplace or elsewhere is
  essential today. Internal decisions need to
  be made much more quickly, implementation of
  decisions needs to be accomplished rapidly.
  To obtain internal approvals, managers should
  not need to feel they are"swimming upstream
  through thick molassas".

  The answer to this problem is to build the
  capacity to remain flexible and responsive
  into the organization so that change can occur

when consumer tastes, competitive technology,
or prices change, and the company must respond in shifts in sourcing, pricing, product strategy, package design, production modifications, or other strategies.

No equipment, for plant or office, should be
purchased unless it is flexible and can respond
to new demands.

No product should be produced that cannot be
differentiated from a standardized base.

No business unit within the firm should be
managed in ridgid ways that do not conform
to the requirements of their tasks. Units
may differ in their management requirements.
Some may be centralized, some decentralized.
Their strategic tasks will differ. Their
levels of complexity and scope will vary, and
their necessity of responsiveness to local
conditions will vary.

. although the new flexibility is mandatory in
a competitive organization, the organization
must remain stable and part of a whole. Top
management must make certain that the firm is
continually in balance...in a state of equi-
librium, and that no one part dominates others.

When properly managed, the diversity of perceptions, interests, and abilities can add
greatly to corporate competitiveness goals.
To this end, top management must provide that
vision..."X" factor...that will draw key
managers together in a shared commitment to
corporate strategy. Values, philosophy, and
key strategies must be internalized.

To get this commitment, complex firms now
operating in a fast changing world often
rely on control systems, centralized management, or training in a common culture and
shared perspective which insures that decisions made will be the "right" decisions,
based on corporate values and interests.

In a balanced organization, attention is
given to the major segments of central staff,
products, geographic considerations, and
other major dimensions.

. inadequate control when corporation is under
competitive marketplace threat. Under these
circumstances a combination of adjustments
may need to be made, i.e.
    more information sent to top management.
    more delegation of decision-making to
          unit, region,
    allocation of resources to unit and hold
          them strictly accountable for results,
    employ profit oriented independent managers.
    new structures or mechanisms to improve
          flow of resources, performance monitor-
          ing against budget goals, motivating
          of performance through incentives,
    tightening of financial controls,
    continued availability of centralized in-
          formation, and expertise.
    more emphasis on cooperation between units
          in which the end result may be to the
          mutual advantage of all those cooper-
          ating, such as in a cooperative market-
          ing project geared to a major region.

. inadequate attention to corporate processes,
in addition to structure. The way decisions
and formal recommendations are made within
the firm can be critical. This and other

process issues need to be examined at the appropriate level, globally, at headquarters, regionally, or locally.

- the careful use of coordinative mechanisms in addition to integrative emphases. Coordinative efforts can bring units together to solve problems with created synergies. Groups can come together for short projects, rather than the permanent meshing of work, but care must be taken that they are both efficient and effective in financial cost and in time consumed. Power grabs must not be allowed to occur.

- inadequate use of corporate networks can make the firm less competitive. The firm must be perceived as a whole. Even though units may be highly differentiated around the globe or nation, each should actually be contributing a unique specialization or complementary resource to the total organization. The weaving of parts of the organization into a fabric of shared tasks and joint responsibilities when needed can assist in threat situations. Key personnel on all levels must be both globally sensitive and locally responsive.

Many advanced firms today are becoming even more self sufficient, expanding their own local networks to include distributors and plants, with multi-level communication channels back to headquarters.

In a competitive firm, there should not be totally independent units or businesses, each should contribute to the whole.

Corporate networks can offer the best source
for each input so that the greatest efficiency is obtained. Where are the best resources ? Where is the most advantageous place
to manufacture? Where assemble? Structure
must be placed to greatest advantage around
the globe, region, or nation. Through role
differentiation , national subsidiaries and
regional units can respond to global tasks.

. corporate strategies must be seen as part of
a long range systematic plan, in which development of units is monitored. A typical
example is a strategy of one firm for
expanding globally:

First a small sales unit is established.
Second, the unit is expanded to include
    technicians and engineering support for
    products.
Then direct control of distribution is taken.
Factories are set up to better reach local
    markets, which helps solve import and
    export currency problems.
Competent locals are hired and retained to
    deal with local political and other
    problems .
Adjustments, permitted under a flexible
    system, are made for best strategy.
Information about competitors, and monitor-
    ing for market opportunities is key to
    staying several steps ahead of competi-
    tors.

Problems in organizations are infinite in their
variety. Each depends on an analysis and individual circumstances for a solution. But most
involve either structure or process barriers
which greatly impede competitiveness.

Considerations in Restructuring an Organization

As we have seen, pressures from low cost competitors in all major markets in the U.S., Europe. and
Asia today have led many firms to restructure as
a first major step in gaining competitiveness.
Loss of market share, mostly to Japanese firms,
has turned the spot light on corporate ineffi -
ciences and ineffectiveness in procedures and
management in many firms.

The resulting necessary restructuring has too
often been painful. Not only WHAT is done, but
the WAY in which it is accomplished has impli-
cations for decades to come, since the effects
of slash and burn techniques destroy organization and morale and hold the corporation back
from its goal of becoming a revitalized and
competitive corporation,

In restructuring the firm, take no steps until
an analysis has been done of the competitor's
advantage in your industry. Then start with a
compensation for your deficiencies in those areas
first.

In general, plan to change as little as possible.
Reinforce existing capabilities and advantages
that exist in the firm now. If possible, upgrade
further develop, and give added responsibility
to existing units first. Then add or delete
from the structure and processes as may be advantageous. Keep every existing advantage you
have; don't let morale deteriorate .

Be certain the structure and processes are flexible and can be changed or modified to take advantage of new opportunities or to refocus for a
closer fit with strategy.

Any changes that are made should be made at the
same time you are keeping current performance
up to its highest level.

When change is the best procedure, build as many
processes as possible into the shifts, so that
there will be greater acceptance and understanding of the need for the changes. Participation
techniques have been important in this regard,
but will be time consuming.

When restructured , refocused and reshaped
operations , which are differentiated, should be
viewed as part of a whole framework which is
integrated for maximium effectiveness and efficiency .

To design the competitive organization, the areas
considered below must be considered:

- does the organization structure and processes
  contribute to the goals of competitiveness,
  profits, productivity, and performance, or
  do they block their attainment? Company
  objectives should be clear.

- what are the major competitive pressures?

- what is the time framework involved?

- what geographic elements, such as cultural and
  political considerations, need to be taken into
  account?

- analyze work needed, including management,
  creative, and production. What tasks are needed, how can the work best be done, how much

can technology contribute to competitiveness
in specific areas, and how much added expertise should be added to the work force ?

. what facilities, plant, and equipment are
needed?

. what technical and other systems are needed?
Are procedures obsolete or are they taking
too much time or bogging managers down in redundancy and paper work?

. what controls are needed and how much control?
Controls should be exercised in all key areas
such as financial and accounting areas, production areas, personnel areas, and marketing
areas of costs, sales performance, and
customer satisfaction.

. what integration links need to be established
to best accomplish work tasks, i.e. research
→manufacturing→marketing; with suppliers and
distributors, with other firms in global or
domestic alliances? Where is integration responsibility? What issues related to power
and conflict need to be resolved?

. is the entire structure and processes efficient? Is the least work done in the most
efficient way? Efficiency is essential to
the competitiveness of the firm.We want the
most output for the least input of any kind.

. does the structure and systems meet the
essential criteria of workability? Is it the
best way to get the <u>results</u> the company
seeks?

Other factors affecting competitiveness follow.

CHAPTER IV
MAXIMIZING PRODUCTIVITY

In the search for competitiveness and strong profits, cost cutting measures and reorganization
have made many firms competitive in world markets.
However, this edge is being sapped by internal
factors such as higher labor compensation, and the
need for advanced skills training. To keep costs
contained within the firm, productivity improvements will need to continue to be made. Even
further, to sustain competitiveness, many firms
will need to maximize their productivity even
further.

Productivity, often related negatively as"driving
workers to produce more", should be seen as a
means to competitiveness ...of benefit to all in
the firm.

The Productivity Challenge

Productivity is an indicator of economic efficiency.
To be competitive, a corporation or a nation must
be productive, efficient, and effective.

Although America, or any individual firm may have
a high ratio of productivity, the growth of productivity over time may be slower than that of
its major competition. Thus, the United States
finds itself lagging behind the Japanese in productivity growth.

This condition is especially serious when other lacks can be readily seen, such as a lack of innovation, and a lack of speed in production processes necessary to get quality products to market at a low cost.

The seriousness of low productivity can be seen in the decline of American productivity growth from 3+% to 1+% per year. This slower growth in output per hour leads to a slower growth in wages and hence in buying power and standard of living.

Although manufacturing productivity has rebounded to about 3% recently, that gain is largely due to downsizing efforts, reductions in work force, and unit and plant closings. Overall, most economists project a modest average gain of about 2.5% for the 1990's.

Although there are numerous other factors in the productivity situation nationally, ...such as our balance of payments, budget deficit, trade barrier problems...the U.S. must not lose sight of the fact that it is now the world's largest debtor nation. The national situation is a compex one. However, within the individual corporation much can be done by various simultaneous actions.

Productivity is important to business because it will improve profits, increase dollar market share by increasing sales, reduce costs, and help provide better service to customers. More profit helps provide money for investment and growth, which means jobs expansion.

Labor is interested in increased productivity as a control on job loss due to imports from competitors.

Government sees productivity as necessary to
eliminate trade deficits and balance budgets.

While, for individuals, productivity means new
jobs creation, raising standard of living, and
in many cases, more job satisfaction.

Companies with poor productivity are companies
that are poorly managed. Low productivity is
generally conceded to be an internal organization weakness primarily.

It is always combined with other problems, such as
  . difficulty in coping with change, technology,
    or discontinuity.

  . poor quality and high costs

  . decreasing profits, sales volume, and market
    share .

  . time delays and late delivery.

  . ineffective managers.

  . uncoordinated and fragmented internal systems
    and programs.

  . low employee and manager morale.

  . obsolete plant and equipment.

  . poor information and communication systems.

  . low producing research and development.

  . inadequate strategic planning and incorrect
    priorities .

. inefficient or redundant work processes.

. inadequate training,

. poor morale and low use of motivation.

External reasons for low productivity vary within industries. However, the macro issues are clearly intense international competition on product price and quality from Japan, W. Germany, Korea, Taiwan, and others.

Also playing a significant role are the factors of the sluggish global economy, low capital spending by customers, a weakness in major markets, the strong U.S. dollar, the enormous federal deficit which keeps interest rates high and retards economic growth, regulatory issues, dips in cyclical businesses, union restrictions on work which does not permit competitive productivity standards, high employment costs, and trade area problems.

Of the many problems identified above, the most serious are:

. internally, the inadequate management depth in productivity and competitiveness areas, and uncoordinated and fragmented or conflicting internal systems.

. externally, the problem of high competition and related market share and profits problems.

We have stated previously that the goal of competitiveness is of great importance to corporations today if they wish to survive; and that the first priority goal of any firm must be profit maximization. Productivity is one key to organizational performance.

<u>**Productivity Defined**</u>

To maximize productivity, it must first be defined.

Any total organization can be defined as a pro -
duction system. Productivity is a way to measure
the effectiveness and efficiency of any production
system in which work processes change materials
from one form to another, which is the result desired. In other words, the process by which inputs ,(usually materials) are converted by work
processes into outputs,(results), are measured by
productivity...which has the goal of getting a
given result with the resources available at the
lowest cost.

To be competitive, corporations today must produce high quality, low cost products, made with
state-of-the-art technology, by highly trained
and well motivated personnel.

As previously stated, in business, total organization measures are financial, as measured by
accounting information, plus the criteria of size
and growth. Comparisons are made within industries
which indicate how well as company is doing.

On the department or unit level, measures can be
objective, such as direct costs, counts or ratios,
or subjective , such as general descriptions of
the degree of satisfaction, or judgemental, on a
scale of 1-10.

Measures must be valid and accurate so they can
reflect changes. They must be complete, including
all inputs and outputs in all activities, and
they must be comparable so that changes in productivity can be measured between time periods.

They must provide feedback in a timely way, and
must themselves be cost-effective.

In the management of productivity, we want to make
all corporate work productive by systematically
focusing on performance and results. The end result may be a product, a service, information, or
knowledge work. Measurements made at critical
points in a work-flow process should be the way
an organization keeps score of how well it is
doing. Measures themselves will provide a motivating role by establishing goals and targets.

Of the three production system factors, the inputs and the work processes are cost items. The
third factor, outputs, is revenue producing.

Profits are maximized when each part of the business is operating near maximum productivity, and
the total result of coordinating or integrating
individual parts produces a final output that is
better than could have been produced individually.

Productivity is usually described according to
ratios such as: per labor hour, per unit of
material, or per unit of capital. Each ratio is,
in turn, influenced either positively or negatively by numerous other factors, such as:

  . the managerial or union limits set on pro-
    ductivity.

  . the policies, procedures, and methods used
    within the firm.

  . the performance group norm level of managers
    and workers.

  . the materials provided.

. the scale of operations.

. resource capacities.

. rate of technical superiority, and others.

$$\frac{\text{Total output}}{\text{Total input}} = \frac{\text{Total results}}{\text{Total consumed}} = \frac{\text{Effectiveness}}{\text{Efficiency}}$$

The ratio of outputs to inputs reflects the efficiency by which resources are transferred into outputs.

Inputs include the cost of materials, the amount of human labor, technology and tools, etc.

Outputs include the number of products or services produced, their quality and their market value.

Productivity Maximized

Since the factors which affect productivity are complex, the job of maximizing productivity is a challenge.

In this context we are concerned about two basic elements in the productivity system, they are:

. operating efficiency, which is relatively high output in relation to minimal input, or how well we achieve our results, and

. organizational effectiveness, which is the actual achievement of desired goals or results, such as tying a group's performance to organizational goals and manager accountability.

The three basic ways that organizations can make
productivity gains then are by:

. maintaining the same level of output while reducing input of worker hours or resources
  consumed.

. increasing the output while maintaining the
  same level input.

. increasing output while decreasing the input.

Increasing production by increasing inputs, i.e.
of labor, capital or others, is NOT productivity.

Related ways firms are attempting to raise productivity are by job redesign, training, participation practices, better product quality, use of
new technology, new management information systems, new motivational techniques, simplification
of work flow and procedures, and many others.

Maximizing productivity is basically the answer to
the question of how much output can be raised in
a given work unit of any kind...plant, clerical,
managerial, or knowledge worker. The answer can be
estimated in three ways:

. keep productivity records. Measure and compare
  the average productivity of a work unit with
  its own highest productivity level, or with
  the productivity of a similar group under same
  conditions. Multinational firms often use this
  technique, when they intentionally duplicate
  plant conditions in two countries for compar-
  ison.

. break the work of one unit into basic steps,

time each step, and allow for minimum breaks.
Determine high production and normal output
in a standard interval of time.

  • identify performance that is the most de -
    sirable and the least desirable, and work
    for the middle for an acceptable high pro-
    ductivity standard for a single unit.

Consider also the two related factors of quality
and control of work, which are related closely to
productivity.

  • quality is generally defined as giving the
    customer the product or result they want,
    in accordance with previously specified
    standards for that product, on time. A high
    quality product or service allows a company
    to increase its market share and raise prices.
    As a key to competitiveness, quality has
    been receiving much attention in American
    firms and others.

    Quality can be improved at the basic work
    unit by first defining quality, based on
    customer expectations. Then set standards,
    design and implement an evaluation process,
    include procedures related to quality in the
    training program, design and implement mea-
    sures, and evaluate results.

    Typical measures for quality include the
    number of rejects, repeat work items, the
    frequency and severity of complaints from
    customers, and quality assurance check
    scores.

    In another sense, the quality of the work
    itself , accomplished within a single unit,

should also be a concern. The objective here
is to complete the work task correctly the
first time it is done, with subsequent savings
in time for the worker and the supervisor,
in addition to the benefit of greatly in -
creased productivity capacity and reduction
in production costs.

. control involves establishing standards for
a given task and then maintaining them with a
constant or check-point feedback mechanism
and corrective action.

The focus of the control function should be
on the work and not the worker. The control
system itself should be minimal in cost, so
benefits are not outweighed.

Control systems are most often used in manufacturing, but the concept can and should be
applied to all other work that is complex in
content. Diverse tasks can be identified and
a productive sequence established, with controls.

Productivity in an Individual Unit

In the simpliest form, productivity is concerned
with how the individual performs given work tasks,
how quickly he does it, and how well he does it.
Likewise, we are basically concerned with one
manager and the employees he supervises, plus the
work and rate of productivity of his unit.

One suggested procedure for maximizing productivity
in a single operating unit is summarized in the
following steps:

(1) review the corporate mission and goals , as
    well as department objectives based on goals.

(2) think through priorities, level of acceptable
    results, measures of performance, and all
    timing and deadlines factors.

(3) design a simple flow-chart of the steps in-
    volved in each operation within the depart-
    ment or unit; analyze for rational sequence
    in order to obtain the most efficient per-
    formance. Remove barriers. Develop alter-
    natives.

(4) put individual operations together into a
    sequential production process, considering
    quality and quantity factors, resources
    needed, machines and tools to be provided
    or improved, changes in policies or pro-
    cedures needed, and training required. There
    may also be other unique requirements need-
    ed for that specific situation.

    Special attention should be paid to the
    linking points where operations overlap and/
    or flow together. Check for delays, dupli-
    cation of effort or other lack of effic-
    iency.

(5) choose best alternatives, after testing,
    and forecast productivity gains anticipated.
    Check results with both quantitative and
    qualitative measures.

(6) give feedback to employees on how well they
    are doing. Identify unsatisfactory perfor-
    mance or procedures and correct.

The productivity of any single individual job
should be measured in accordance with the procedure outlined previously for maximizing productivity. Every job has an optimum capacity
which can be identified. Both quantitative and
qualitative measures should be applied.

Productivity gains, in order to have the most
meaning for the corporation, should be translated
into dollars. Improvements in productivity should
be noted and rewards given for performance in some
way. Care should be taken however, that gains at
the lower levels have meaning for employees in
terms of their immediate job. Quoting large financial investment figures alone will not have
meaning for the average worker.

Productivity Keys and Strategies

The key to maximizing productivity in the organization is the overall performance level of the
managers and employees within their total work
environment. Productivity problems can be traced
to incompetent managers, faulty employee selection processes, lazy employees, inadequate training, poor motivation, inefficient or ineffective
work processes, obsolete plant and equipment,
lack of effectively functioning vertical and
horizontal organization structures, poor company
controls, and incorrect priorities.

How much real support is the manager and employee
given by the organization structure, policies, and
procedures , both formal and informal, within which
work is done?

To attain productivity optimization in the whole
organization, the company must attain maximim
productivity in EACH BASIC OPERATING UNIT, which

is the nuts and bolts of productivity in any organization. Each unit needs to be carefully designed
and analyzed for procedures, workflow, and linking
points, after first having established space,
machines, and equipment. Each unit should have the
goal of obtaining total potential results, within the money, materials, and controls made available to it.

In times of intense competition and inflation
combined with a sluggish world market, each firm
must minimize human resource utilization and still
meet and surpass corporate goals.

A corporate appraisal of its productivity progress toward maximization can be made by obtaining
the answers to the following questions. Determine:

- the percent of reduction in the rework rate.

- the number of customer complaints. Decreased?

- reduction in unit costs? How much?

- reduced man hours per unit? How many?

- reduced cost of materials?

- reduced product costs and price?

- reduced number of days lost through strikes?

- reduced employee turnover rate?

- reduced number of union grievance cases?

- reduced number of product recalls?

Plus, have you attained:

. increased savings from employee suggestions?

. improved your products in quality areas?

. improved your relationships with your suppliers
  or distributors, making them feel a part of
  your company team?

. a faster product development cycle?

. improvements from the new technology your
  company purchased for plant, office, or the
  communications needs of the firm?

. improvements from innovations in administration, research, manufacturing, marketing,
  processes ?

. improvements from human resource innovations
  such as efficient participatory techniques?

. improvements due to tighter controls, such as
  cost controls, resource allocation, efficient purchasing, maximization of resource
  capacity, and inventory control to minimize
  excessive costs or shortages.

. increased savings directly attributable to
  new alliances or cooperative agreements with
  outside businesses or organizations in
  manufacturing, research, or other areas?

. has your investment in basic research, plant
  or equipment paid off?

Human resources and productivity has already been
identified as a critical area , since it is how
people perform that determines the productivity
level.

Individual managers and workers affect productivity in two ways:

. by better and smarter behavior on the job,
  which directly contributes to the goals and
  objectives of competitiveness in the firm.

. by following the best identified practices of
  the firm in areas such as costs and efficiency.

Attitude and skills are both important keys to the
behavior of the individual, but there are also
other equally important considerations in getting
the right people in the right jobs.

Recruit people with the skills you want, so that
a minimum of training is necessary. Job previews
with potential employees should be realistic and
not sugar-coated, especially regarding the firm's
culture, salary expectations, and chances for
advancement. Dissatisfaction with a misrepresented
job will cause a poor attitude later and the
employee will not be of benefit to the firm.

In the selection process, include tests if they
are thought to be valid. Research has shown that
test-selected employees outperform non-test-select-
ed employees by almost 10%. When hundreds of
workers are involved, this can mean a substantial
savings to the corporation over time. Psychologi-
cal tests, intelligence tests, and aptitude tests,
can be use together with interviews.

Once the employee has been hired, it is essential
that he understand his job and the broader focus
of the firm. Training should include :

. training in productivity, new skills, and specific behaviors of best job performance. Include both managers and workers.

  Illustrate productivity and performance on the
  job through models to clarify best practices.

  The performance of any individual is influenced
  directly by the goal norms established for-
  mally or informally by the individual, his
  work group, and his supervisor...in some cases
  also his union representative. A concensus
  of these elements must be acknowledged as
  fundamental to productivity dimensions in the
  organization, and upper limits raised , or
  there will be very little increase in productivity. This is a critical factor in some
  firms, and almost nonexistant in others.

  Some job redesign may be found necessary.

. evaluation and feedback on performance is
  essential to productivity improvement. Since
  about 70% of the work force have jobs that
  are not easily measurable as output per man
  hour, such as managerial or white collar,
  it is suggested that a results focused approach
  (management-by-objectives) be used to determine the quantity and quality of all work
  done· A commitment to these results,based on
  corporate and unit goals, will focus personal
  energy and increase productivity.

. motivational techniques that have been proven

successful with productivity payoffs include:

- .¯ goal setting for quantity and quality
  outputs. Link goals in the employees mind
  with performance standards and the larger
  unit and total corporate goals.

- .financial incentives can lead to increased
  productivity, if dependent upon the performance of the individual or group, or
  total organization performance.

- . participation in many different forms can
  increase productivity and organizational
  performance. Must be controlled for
  efficiency and evaluated for outcomes.
  Results as a productivity motivator are
  mixed.

- . other rewards that have meaning for most
  managers and employees as motivators are
  social activities or status rewards. The
  key is to determine what motivates particular employees to greater productivity
  and commitment, then let them share in
  those rewards.

Productivity is seen by many workers as a threat.
They think they are literally working themselves
out of a job if fewer workers can do the work of
many. Security in employment is therefore a
prime motivator for many today. This aspect will
need to be addressed if there are to be any productivity gains in office or plant floor.

Human resource policies and training should pro-
mote continuous learning, innovation and creativity in all areas, teamwork, participation and

flexibility, in addition to the techniques that
have been previously identified.

Direction from top corporate leadership is
necessary to establish overall motivation and
provide the missing "X" factor which will mean
maximum employee commitment to company goals.

Non-Manufacturing areas and Productivity

In corporations today, non-manufacturing areas,
such as offices, are among the last to be analyzed
for productivity patterns, and what has been done
has been largely inconclusive.

There is a substitution of computers and word
processors for clerical and sales workers in many
firms, with a monitoring of productivity by
the machines themselves. This trend is causing
many problems in some firms, and should be applied
with caution.

Office systems themselves require their own integration today, i.e the flow of information
between different functions, ability to run different functions at different levels of workstation
and department, and multi-vendor integration.

Productivity improvements can be made by examining
the work being done and how it flows. Simplify
and eliminate excess paper work if possible. Redesign physical layouts and eliminate barriers
and problems to efficiency. Evaluate any savings
due to increased productivity. Then seek further
productivity gains by the careful selection of
technology, which should be flexible and user
friendly. Policies regarding employee use of
technology should be guided by current findings
on health factors, which can prove costly for the
firm and for the employees.

Manufacturing areas and Productivity

There has been a sense of renewed importance for
manufacturing in the pursuit of competitiveness
in American based firms and around the globe.

Production systems are associated with both manufacturing systems and service systems, in which
management tries to get the best utilization of
company resources by coordinating and integrating
materials, machines, and human resources for
productivity and profits. In fact many firms
have applied productivity standards to manufacturing and not yet to the company as a whole.

Typical steps in instituting a productivity
emphasis in production are:

- benchmark the competition in terms of products, policies, markets, processes, and
  distribution.

- On the basis of this analysis, decide on what
  basis your company will compete. There is a
  choice between high profit margins on product
  price which leads to low market share, or
  high output volumes which can respond more
  easily to cost reduction pressures.

- In the area of quality, you can compete to
  provide higher quality on a standardized
  product, or provide features or performance
  that is unique.

- Your firm can compete on product dependa -
  bility, or on product flexibility, or other
  dimensions.

- How you compete should give you a market edge.

. appraise company skills and resources. Manufacturing must be consistent with total
corporate strategy. Only then can management gain efficiency without wasting resources by making improvements in areas that
make no difference in terms of corporate
goals. Experts in manufacturing specialities,
from technology, to engineering, to labor
should all be involved.

The focus should be on products. Variables
to be considered revolve around cost, time,
quality and quantity, technological con-
straints, customer satisfaction. While decisions will need to be made in the areas
of plant and equipment, production planning
and control, labor and staffing, product
design and engineering, organization and
management.

Key questions include how we can best set
up manufacturing tasks to meet goals in
the most efficient way? What are the barriers
to success? What do we lack?

. integration of manufacturing with other
functions is part of the process. Firms that
have difficulty in this area need company
culture reinforcement and training in teams
and other participatory decision-making groups.
Aim for speed in product development, and
responsiveness to fast changing markets.
Although emphases may vary, the integrated
strategy should produce parallel improvements
in cost...keep it low, in quality...keep it
high , and in delivery... keep it fast and
reliable.

Other suggestions to improve production productivity are:

- in any process involving several different functions, focus a team effort on the results desired, such as a certain market cost, and work backward to design and produce that product at that cost. This will save time and money in rethinking and redesigning unacceptable products.

- production processes themselves should allow as much flexibility as possible , so that adaptions can be made to changing markets.

- within the production process itself, develop measures and techniques to monitor and improve the efficiency of the process.

- use cutting edge technology for strategic advantage.

- emphasize product variety, available at market faster, at low cost and high quality for maximum customer satisfaction. This emphasis requires integration between research, product development, production, and marketing.

- institute adequate production controls over total volume of production, necessary for purchasing materials, employment, finance, and other, and the detailed planning and control of detailed operations day to day through routing, scheduling, dispatching, and follow-up.

- innovate in production processes .

. scan the world for resources and materials.

.- train employees for more than one job,
  and in use of technology.

.when satisfactory production processes are
 in place, fine-tune them even more. Make
 improvements in all aspects a continuous
 task.

. within similar plants, productivity rates
  vary. What are the barriers to production
  in each plant? Labor relations ? Is the
  focus of the plant too broad and unmanagea-
  ble in products, technologies, volumes, and
  markets? Is work force unmotivated? Are
  management practices prople-oriented and
  include participation? Are the people
  being hired inadequate?

  Why should productivity be improved? Is
  there motivation for improvement, and
  accurate monitoring and assessment of
  progress?

  Is there too much internal competition?
  Are interfunctional linkages breaking down?

Significant reduction in costs of production will
benefit from a continuous-flow, waste-free production system, using just-in-time techniques.

There are many examples of excellent corporate
productivity programs that have yielded results
and are being continuously improved. As new
techniques are adopted by corporations striving
for best practices, the productivity competitiveness battles in the future will increasingly
be won on the total effectiveness of management
and organizational design.

CHAPTER V
MAXIMIZING PERFORMANCE

Company performance is the overview result of all
corporate efforts. Profit is the single best result that indicates that the company is doing the
things it should do to get positive results. Size
and growth are additional major indicators of performance.

In evaluating company performance, there are
various established areas which must be considered
simultaneously, thus giving an integrated performance picture of the firm. These areas are
mission and strategy, internal organization,
information and data, company culture, and human
resources.

1) In the mission and strategy area, how well
   has the company defined its mission and how
   good is the"fit"between the key strategy of
   of the corporation, the key strategy in the
   industry that will mean success, and the
   ability of the firm to support and implement
   that strategy ?

   The ability to strategically analyze the
   competitive environment for a specific industry and company in a specfic geographic
   location, at a particular time, must also
   have timely and strong implementation within the firm.

For example, where competitive success is
seen as exploiting changing technology in
the industry with new products, before it is
recognized by other firms, the company emphasis will be on gaining the technology,
securing distribution, and ear-marking cash
flow for fast action when indicated. One of
these newly emerging areas is micro machines.

In another example, where industry competitive success is seen as dependent on the key
of local responsiveness to the consumer, the
firm will decentralize its units for sensitivity to local markets or regions and for
awareness of new opportunities. The internal
organization policies and procedures will
need to be geared to facilitate this strategy.

Determining the right strategy is only the
first step to successful performance. But
without the right strategy, the company will
be uncompetitive.

Strategies are often patterned after military
moves, some among them are the frontal attack,
flanking, encirclement, bypass attack, or
guerrila warfare.

2) Internal organization. If the corporation has
   the right strategy for the industry and for
   the characteristics of the business, but
   cannot support and implement the strategy
   internally in a committed way, the company
   will be uncompetitive.

   To do this, additional key goals need to be
   woven into procedures and accountabilities

throughout the company in ways that support
the strategy. Some of these key goals may be
efficiency, productivity, quality, innovation, global product leadership, and gaining major market share. To attain these
goals, further actions are necessary within
the firm, as identified in the preceeding
chapters of this book.

For example, to gain major market share,
low prices for products are thought to be
necessary, which is based on low cost production. To get low cost production, various
other changes will be needed, probably in
technology, organization of layout and work,
design,and marketing and human relations
areas.

In attaining internal policies and procedures
that actively support key strategy and
goals, the focus must be on RESULTS that must
be obtained. Actions intended to obtain these
results should be analyzed for efficiency
and cost-effectiveness themselves.

In addition, procedures and processes that
require cooperation, linking, and integration should be analyzed for both results
effectiveness and for efficiency as a process or procedure itself.

To facilitate communication and results,
some firms today are establishing linking
in some form on several levels of the
company at the same time.

The importance of integration can readily
be seen when the sequence of events in a

company seeking competitiveness invests in
cutting-edge high technology equipment,
which leads to greater production, but the
customers for the greater number of products are not there and the plant has excess
capacity which means cutbacks in employment.
The marketing input has been absent in the
planning stages, and no marketing thrust was
mounted in the latter stages.

The most essential integration usually lies
between research→manufacturing→marketing.
In the overview, the three elements of
geography, products, and function should all
be integrated together.

Research is the basis for product line renewal. It creates new options and innovative
products essential to performance in the
marketplace. The essential pressure on research is the very short-to-market time now
required for competitiveness. Fast action
and accurate assessment of potential for
market must be part of an efficient and
smooth process. An emphasis on user-friendly
equipment or products using environmentally
safe materials are a new challenge, together
with choices in production methods.

Manufacturing competitiveness requires some
access to capital for advanced technology
and automated manufacturing processes. It
should show a return-on-assets great enough
to permit growth. Plant capacity should be
utilized effectively and operating efficiencies increased. Production cost reductions hinges on continuous flow, waste-
free and flexible manufacturing capacities.

Marketing and sales organizations must be
in close working relationships with manufacturing, usually with an efficient logistics system providing fast and reliable
supplies of products throughout the globe.

The thrust of marketing is now to provide
a quality product, usually at low cost, to
customer niches that want that product. The
addition of the provision of service appli-
cations and know-how to customers is
especially important in areas like technology.

Mass marketing, although declining in favor
of customized segments, can still be effective if sufficient flexibility is built into
products to provide variation.

Marketing should communicate with research
and development on the importance of
commercialization to the profit motive to
the firm.

It is essential in analyzing the various
organizational elements for performance
that a flexibility of response be built into
all systems, including decision-making,
administrative, information system, and
all coordinating systems. This means that
different parts of the organization can be
structured differently to meet different
needs in the organization. Some are more
complex, some need more authority and responsibility and some less, some firms need
maximum support for market competitiveness,
while others who hold a dominant market
position need to combat apathy with internal
competition and job shifts.

The performance of each system can be

maximized by changing what is not effective.

An organization systems approach permits the
most effective results to be obtained by
designing a total corporate system in which
each part relates to every other part. Such
a system provides focus and pulls together
and tightens up all segments of the organization into results-oriented total syn -
chronized performance using controls within each system and at each level to monitor
performance.

After policies, procedures, and systems are set
and integrated and monitored for best results,
they should be fine-tuned for even better performance. The improvement process, the monitoring
and evaluation of internal structure and processes must be ongoing, with the emphasis on
moving upward continually.

The principle criteria to use in evaluating the
performance of a competitive internal system
is:

  . does it support the corporate strategy and
    facilitate the achievement of results?

  . does it work quickly, efficiently, and effec-
    tively?

As part of the corporate system, Boards of
Directors will need to set-up their own criteria
for judging and improving their results in the
discharge of their duties to the corporation.

(3) Information is basic to competitive per-
    formance. The firm relies on data in essen-
    tial ways. Information must be gathered
    shrewdly and used very quickly to be use-
    ful on identification of market trends,
    competitor moves, and new opportunities.

    Does your firm have adequate competitor
    and other information ? It is a major
    factor in your competitive performance.

    At most firms competitor information is
    both weak and fragmented. Usually collect-
    ed informally, it is not centralized and
    is not available throughout the firm. How-
    ever,when it is sent up to a superior,
    the resulting review can add a new pro-
    duct line, new pricing, or new strategy.

    The most desirable data, and the most
    difficult to obtain are on product in-
    come and sales, market strategy, pro-
    duction costs, and future growth and
    strategies. Advance information is es-
    pecially useful and some companies do
    maintain offices around the globe for the
    purpose of scanning for such information
    and opportunities.

    At the same time, managers need an in-
    house data base on their industry and com-
    petition for quick analysis of financial
    trends, summary of marketing and manufact-
    uring activities, market share, product
    development priorities, market strategies,
    and acquisition studies.

    There is an interest in any other area

that gives the competitor an edge, such as
production processes, technology, strategy
and others.

Much material comes from already published
reports such as the annual report, which
gives gross sales and balance sheet/ income
statement ratios, and market analysis. It is
difficult to get information from foreign
field offices, but this is a source that
should not be overlooked.

Management information systems (MIS) for
decision making is very important to competitiveness. Managers must obtain the information they need and then know how to utilize
it to the best advantage. To operate effectively, the information system must provide
the necessary information, analyze operations,
and perform profit maximization techniques.
Subsystems for all major areas should be included, such as finance, personnel, purchasing, marketing, and management.

Company culture.
The way work is done, the characteristics
of the company in the minds of the people
who work there, strongly influence their
corporate performance. Do they see the firm
as dynamic and fast moving or staid and slow
to take advantage of opportunities? Culture
is a mix of policies, procedures, and
systems that guide preferred behavior. Firms
that want competitive performance must
create a climate which leads to dynamic
commitment to goals, achievement and results.

(4) Manager and employee performance.
     In order to attain and sustain a high per-
     forming and competitive corporation, the
     competitive stratgy and values must be in-
     stitutionalized. All policies, procedures,
     processes, and rewards must reflect com-
     petitiveness values.

     Managers and employees are the major key
     to competitiveness. Their collective per-
     formance makes a difference; their indi-
     vidual performance as decision-makers
     makes a difference. Decisions which disre-
     gard efficiency, workers who slow down
     work when a new technology is introduced,
     or whole units that are at war with other
     divisions instead of cooperating with them
     on vital company matters, are all examples
     of a failure of the high performing com-
     petitive philisophy of the company. It is
     basic that, when he is hired, every em-
     ployee must understand the corporate
     values, his job, and how it relates to the
     whole system.

     Managers themselves must be results or-
     iented toward the accomplishment of cor-
     porate goals. They must:

     . keep a positive attitude through a
       variety of internal changes designed
       to make the firm more successful. This
       is not always easy, but is essential.

     . regard every change, including restruc-
       turing, as building onto existing or-
       ganizational competencies to refocus

them more effectively in a shifting and
rough and tumble environment.

. accept the need to perform efficiently,
effectively, and productively as their individual management responsibility.

. accept the need to perform in cooperation
with others in a coordinated way, integrating where necessary, in order to utilize
corporate resources of all kinds in the
most efficient way, networking on a global
or domestic scope.

. internalize corporate competitive values
in their own management work, and see that
the ideas are carried forward throughout
the firm, including the focused goal
orientation, productivity, efficiency, and
effectiveness.

. improve performance in their own units by
such means as planning priority goals and
objectives, organizing jobs efficiently,
comparing their units productivity and processes with competitors. Determine how to
make further improvements, scan costs and
lower them, make products better and cheap-
er, establish measures, evaluate, improve,
reward for achievement of goals. He or she
should also encourage a unity of purpose
between employees and the company, hold
meetings at which participation is encouraged for defined purposes, know your
department and your company and how they
function in the corporation. Know your
funding and how your firm makes money.
Select and train workers carefully.

. be administratively innovative, not only to
  solve problems and provide a greater profit margin, but also to "make things work
  better" ...more effectively, efficiently,
  and in a more satisfying way for employees.

. be able to work within a flexible structure
  and processes in which units may be organ-
  ized differently for maximum advantage to
  the firm. This structure may, at times,
  be ambigious. The manager must be able to
  work in a variety of situations without
  feeling undue stress or suffering ill
  health. He must keep himself in top physical and mental shape for high competitive
  stamina, required by the company.

. help seize opportunity by being sensitive
  and responsive to emerging future trends,
  not only in competitors but also in geographic regions, cultures, and governments.
  The manager must then have the ability to
  react appropriately and at top speed.

. see the big corporate picture, become less
  parochial, which will enable more effective
  work with diverse parts of their own organization , utilizing various communication
  channels and methods. Since risk is spread
  more widely today among operations, a
  wider understanding is necessary.

. accept the goal of continuous improvement
  of the company and its processes, and
  also of themselves as managers.

. manage so that competitiveness values pre-

dominate. Hire the right people, get procedures and processes up to maximum standard, gain cooperation throughout the
company when required for work responsi-
blity, handle problems, conflicts, and
change. Know how to communicate vertically
and laterally.

Chief executive and senior manager per -
formance.
The chief executive officer of the corporation is ultimately responsible for total
corporate performance and resulting goals
attainment. It is his job to see that the
company which is somewhat profitable and
somewhat productive, strive to maximize
its potential and give an even better performance.

To do this, the chief executive officer
will be certain that the company has
strategic direction, that the business
units have competitive strategies, that
there is a cohesive whole formed when
all units are integrated or linked, and
that a balance of interests is maintained
so that perspectives remain rational and
power conflict is minimized.

Top management tasks require conceptual,
technical, and human relations skills.

He needs to know how to move the corporation forward , through its problems and
developmental growth cycle, making maximum
profitable progress along the way.

In giving leadership and cohesiveness to

the firm, the executive needs to provide
that "X" factor which will result in a
commitment of the individual employee to
the attainment of corporate goals. Such
motivation or inspiration is rare, but has
been at least partially attained by some
companies.

In total competitiveness areas, the executive
needs to establish timely bench-marks of
performance for financial and other controls,
must know what decisions are being made in
the company, and in general must monitor the
entire organization.

Top management controls the key resource of
capital, both supply and investment, control
of the strategic plan and it's implementation,
and control of the key resource of people.

Top management team members may differ in
management style, from aggressive and de-
manding to relaxed and supportive. But they
all share corporate commitment to values,
and function with competence and self- control in the attainment of business goals.
Maximum performance from top teams is expected without any question.

Within the firm, top managers use manager
movement and promotion to reinforce change
objectives, and to give them experience in
other major divisions to broaden their understanding of the company and its problems.

As with all managers, the top team gets results via people in their own functional
area by establishing objectives, directing

the attainment of those objectives, and
measuring and controlling results.

The criteria for performance of a top management team is usually the consistent ability
to produce results over long periods of time,
and in a variety of assignments. The high
performance standard is a "batting average"
which does allow for minimal mistakes.

The attitude and spirit of performance
should be a positive one, focusing on opportunities, even when solving problems. Achievement of results should be a norm and not
an unusual event.

Good executive performers are those who re-
late their work to that of the whole company, realizing that each executive action,
attitude, and behavior in an organization
depends on and affects other actions. The
top management team must synchronize all
activities at the top.

Evaluation varies for management personnel.
But responsibility for manager performance
lies with the chief executive. He needs an
indepth knowledge of what constitutes
competitive performance at each job level.
A few key performance objectives may be
sufficient to determine how the incumbent is
performing. Is it as well as his opposite
in the competition? Outside consultants
can be helpful in getting performance standards; employee opinion surveys are sometimes
used.

On the basis of evaluation, changes in personnel can be made.

Managers on lower levels are usually evaluated
on a results-oriented basis, against their plan.

Poor management performers and producers by a
results attainment criteria, should be replaced
promptly, for their own good as well as that of
the corporation. People in the wrong jobs tend
to become negative and defensive in behavior,
which affects other employees and situations
involving smooth functioning and productivity.
They exhibit such traits as extreme anxiety,
paranoid and harassed perceptions, rigid and
defensive behavior, and emotionalism.

Another approach to improving manager performance
is to impose strict controls in budget, procedures, and approvals, give close supervision,
realign positions or responsibilities, reorganize
jobs, and use mild coercion.

Some indications of managerial incompetence are:

. rigidity in use of methods that do not work.

. waste of critical resources of money, time,
  people, and materials.

.not gathering data necessary to make strategic
  decisions.

. deliberate distortion of information.

. slow or vacillating decisions.

. failure to exploit an advantage.

. when faced with setbacks, blaming bad luck
  or scapegoating.

. failure to do effective work performance.

In corporations who wish to maximize their performance, evaluation should be done, not against
a corporate plan alone, but against budget goals,
against financial criteria such as return on
sales, and against competitor performance.

Managerial performance seldom waits for a formal
evaluation. They are often continually monitored
during monthly performance meetings with the
chief executive, who sometimes travels half way
around the world to meet them in a total group.
Operating executives are grilled for hours during
these sessions, with their budget figures as a
focus. If there is bad news, their recommendations on how to fix the situation are presented.
Such meetings help insure that a specified
return on sales is made; that the cost of the
products produced is reduced by a specified percent, or that new projects, divisions, or merged
firms are doing well and are profitable. Results
are heavily stressed at such meetings, which
are regarded with stress and even fear by the
operating managers of some firms.

To maximize corporate performance, nothing less
than the entire organization needs to be considered and evaluated according to the competitiveness criteria established. Each unit should be
analyzed and its performance improved.

In the overview, it will aid the organization
in its quest for performance to keep things as
simple as possible and to keep them clear. It
is essential that goals and objectives dealing
with performance be made clear and that plans to
implement them be simple. Decisions should be made
in conformance with the company culture, stressing

performance values.

Although companies differ on the amount of integration required for effective overall performance, all need cooperation and communication.
Conflict should be minimal,and effective total
functioning of the company, with fast and smooth
flowing systems should be the norm. Structure
and processes must support competitiveness.

Finally, attention must be given to people. They
are the ones that will make the company truly
competitive. They function best in a vital and
dynamic atmosphere, which allows them to develop
themselves and assume responsibility. Therefore,
participatory techniques should be a part of an
competitiveness agenda. They must be accountable
for results and evaluated on that basis, up and
down the line. Further, they must be rewarded
for their efforts in ways they appreciate.

Efforts to integrate the corporate strategy into
a whole must be linked at the corporate, unit, and
individual levels. A modified management-by-objectives system is most often used to accomplish this.

Companies who need to upgrade their performance
fast, as in a crisis situation, rely on a few
financial and restructuring techniques to get
immediate improvement. However, this is only
part of the job that must eventually be done to
upgrade performance and to sustain it over time.
Other areas must also be considered a priority.

CONCLUSION

Sustained improvement in performance...getting
better in every way in every quarter...is the
competitiveness challenge for management. Best
practices are themselves moving targets, quickly
adopted by competitors and integrated into their
systems selectively.

However, all corporations have areas where they
are not functioning in their own best interest,
and which would benefit from further work and
improvement. In addition, new developments will
always guarantee new challenges and necessitate
reconsideration of corporate priorities and
structures and procedures.

In general, except for unusual crisis situations,
corporations should seek simultaneous improvements
along the several lines already identified across
the entire firm. In review:

- articulate a visionary strategy of what the
  corporation <u>can</u> do.

- set clear competitively oriented goals and
  prioritize them.

- allocate funds for competitiveness and performance improvements and fix responsibility
  for implementation.

. benchmark the competition, then innovate
  to get additional improvements in any and
  all areas.

. modify the company culture as needed into a
  dynamic and positive one, which will get
  commitment to goals.

. get improved organization, structure, and
  processes. Integrate for better results and
  goal achievement.

. achieve internal consistency among systems.

. introduce new technology into plant and
  office where it is certain to assist in
  upgrading productivity and efficiency improvements.

. require managers to get results themselves.

. require managers to modify their management
  techniques to obtain results along lines
  valued by the corporation.

. do highly selective hiring and improve the
  skills and motivation of employees.

. make the corporate commitment to competitiveness a long term one, with improvement
  plans projected into the future.

. tighten controls in all key areas and monitor
  for results.

. use research and technology for strategic
  advantage, to commercialize products that
  get to market FAST.

- keep everything flexible, but stable and
  in balance at the same time.

- market to meet customer needs with tailored
  products.

- measure, measure, measure...and evaluate
  all major areas.

Raising the competitive level of the firm and
bringing profits, productivity, and performance
nearer optimum levels in the most efficient and
effective ways, through a parallel emphasis in
management...a simultaneous track approach... is
challenging. However, firms that seek competitiveness must rise to this challenge, and will find
the results rewarding!

APPENDIX

The following examples of competitiveness
efforts reflect various approaches to unique
problems.

Merck recognized productivity as a major company
concern in 1980. A task force was appointed at
the top level to study productivity at Merck and
the ways to improve it.

Some of their emphases are:
   .discovering and marketing new products and
    services.

   .finding less expensive ways to make products.

   . substituting less expensive raw materials.

   . conserving energy.

   . making the necessary capital investments
    for efficient plants and equipment.

   . taking advantage of new product lines and
    new markets.

In an emphasis on people, Merck stresses working
smarter not harder, making effective use of
available tools, new procedures to simplify tasks,
saving time, increasing quantity, improving quality.

General Electric sees competitiveness and productivity as the "reindustrialization of America"
and by 1980 had already invested $6 bil to upgrade
productivity capabilities.

GE uses its own factories as worldwide laboratories
for the development of advanced manufacturing
systems, and has a customer base that urgently
feels the need for breakthroughs.

GE's goal is to make the company the most competitive enterprise in the world. To do this they
are shifting the mix of businesses toward high
tech and high growth services, supported by heavy
R & D investment, and an accelerated rate of
acquisitions and divestments of those that no
longer fit the strategy.

Also, there is cost cutting, heavy investments in
productivity, upgrading of core businesses,
and plant and equipment expenditures.

The climate is one of growth and quick movement,
excellence, innovation, creativity, and entre-
preneurship. Expressing their growth concept they
say "While we shrink in non-essentials, our main
goal is to expand".

Few corporations are bigger and none is more
complex than GE. Chairman John F. Welch is nothing
if not controversial, but, regardless of new
creative emphases he has recently launched, his
concern for profits first remains. Currently,GE
questions of competitors "What is the secret of
your success?" How things get done, rather than
what gets done is now being investigated. It
will bear watching for results.

At Ford, to increase profits this major U.S.
automaker has cut costs through reduced personnel and manufacturing, redesigned models with
a customer focus, stressed quality and reliability
within company operations and with their own
suppliers, and have extensively involved hard
working employees through participatory efforts
and profit sharing plans.

Managers are seen as leaders and catalysts. Ford
is also subcontracting overseas to a greater
extent, and is fostering an international out-
look.

Honeywell is a company that has downsized but
is more profitable! It has sold its computer
business in phases over the past four years
to French and Japanese companies. Since 1981
Honeywell's earnings per share have almost doubl-
ed, it's dividends increased 100%, and the stock
has nearly trebled. CEO Reiner says the firm has
a dominant position in several industries.

The company has essentially gone back to its
roots as a world leader in heating, air condi-
tioning, and ventilation controls for homes and
buildings, and in process-control equipment.
But because these businesses are relatively
mature, with small potential for further growth,
the company is forced to be highly efficient and
is keeping a constant eye on costs.

In the interests of improving operating efficiency and slashing overhead, the CFO analyzed
the company financial position and reduced cash
tied up as working capital by over $170 mil in
last two years, dumped marginal businesses, and
purchased own stock.

United Technologies, according to one executive,
is a business that" has succeeded with very
aggressive cost management'.' As far as I'm concerned"it's just managing costs, whether it be more
output per unit of labor costs or whatever".

Controls are in selection and training of personnel, a structure which delegates authority
and responsibility, communication of requirements
for compliance with approved accounting, control,
and business practices throughout the organization, and a program of internal audit.

Proctor & Gamble says the foundation of their
company strategy is the real volume of product
sold and shipped.

Improved margins and reduced spending may maintain growth for awhile without volume, but
long term earnings depend on volume. Competitiveness emphasis is therefore on both new products
and established brands, acquisitions, product
technology changes, packaging improvements, value
added to established products, and penetration
of new geographic markets. One recent new product
is Tartar Control Crest. Research and development
is considered to be the life blood of the company
growth. Cost savings are stressed, as are new
capacity projects.

INDEX

ABOUT THE AUTHOR

Dr. Doris Martin heads a small management consulting firm which emphasizes comprehensive general management. and specializes in productivity and performance, strategic planning, and organization design and function.

Her prior successful experience for over twenty years was in various management positions in business, universities, and government.

She holds a doctorate from Columbia University, an M.S. from Boston University, and a B.S. from New York University.

She is a writer and lecturer on topics related to management. Her books are published by the publishing division of her consulting firm, Martin Management Books, which internally generates publications of interest currently to the business community and those interested in management.